Mind's Shadow

Jaahnvi Chandra

Presentation by *BookLeaf Publishing*

Web: www.bookleafpub.com

E-mail: info@bookleafpub.com

ISBN: 9789358730449

First edition 2023

DEDICATION

To all those who have a love for exploring the
depths of the world through literature

PREFACE

Dear Reader,

I am thrilled to present to you "Mind's Shadow," a collection of poems that delve into the intricacies of the human mind. As a writer and a lover of poetry, I have always been fascinated by the power of language to capture the essence of the human experience. This collection is a reflection of my own journey through life, and my attempts to make sense of the world around me.

"Mind's Shadow" is an exploration of the subconscious mind, and an observation of the world around me. Through poetry, I have attempted to give voice to the often-unseen aspects of the human experience, shining a light on the complexities that make us who we are; and to highlight the minuteness of things we failed to notice. The poems in this collection are deeply personal, and yet I believe that they speak to a universal human experience.

It is my hope that "Mind's Shadow" will inspire readers to explore their own minds, and to embrace the power of introspection and self-discovery. I invite you to take this journey with me, to dive into depths and discover the many facets of the mind's shadow.

Blue Flames

A doll with emotions
Oh how you've toyed with me

I fell in love with the ocean
Calm, serene, blue
All it brought me was destruction

The fifteen flares in his blues had me entranced
One strong tidal,
And your flames had me crumbling

Forbiddingly, blindly walked into your waters
Your creatures.. oh they left me with a diamond
mind

As I ran, your burning napalm skies followed
I can't seem to escape your ocean blue eyes

Eye is the Lens

Phones, cameras, instax, and the likes
We cling to them in our daily lives
As if the world can't exist without a device
To capture moments that fleetingly thrive

Yet in this chase, we forget to be present
We let life slip away like a forgotten scent
Lost in the pursuit of the perfect shot
We miss out on living, on what life has got

We reduce life to a two-dimensional plane
A frame that tells a story, but can't contain
The depth and breadth of what we've seen
The sounds, smells, and feelings in between

And so we find ourselves scrolling through a
screen
Trying to relive what once was, but in vain
As the memories fade like a forgotten dream
Leaving us with a feeling of emptiness and pain

But what if we use our eyes as a camera
To capture life's moments without the drama
To see the world in its vivid hues and tones
And store it in our minds like precious stones

Maybe then we'll remember more
Of the laughter, love, and memories we adore
The moments that make life worth living
That keep us going, that keep on giving

So let's put down our devices and look around
Take a breath, listen to the sounds
Let life unfold in its natural way
And savour each moment, as if it's here to sta

Querencia

A young, naive girl
An elder, dominant guy
Oh how the signs flashed red
Alarms ringing in my head

Yet your mere presence calmed me
Your encouragement gave me strength
Your reassurance comforted me
Your appreciation made me feel wanted

Your words hugged me
Blew soft kisses my way
You accepted me with open arms

You didn't judge my wants
You let me be me
You are it for me
You are my querencia

Ephemeral

5

All things must fade away,
Despite our efforts to delay
Forever is a fleeting display

The world ebbs and flows in impermanence
An irony that's inherent in human experience
With every breath, we shed our former selves
Flux as our constant, a reminder to live in the
present realm
For why worry of future fears, when now is all
we truly delve?

Human existence, a void we often see
Searching for meaning in a world empty
Absurdity engulfs, our purpose unknown
Our own sense of being, must be sown

Our time, a minuscule speck of the past
Mortality's mark, a product that won't last
Years seem eternal, but in truth, they are naught
Insignificant fragments, to the universe's thought

A mere tool, the cosmos knows us to be
Humiliated by our own obscurity
Attachments to impermanence, we must forsake
For nothing will remain, as time will take

Memory Lane

Every night I walk down a different road
But as of late, I have gravitated to the same one
And I think it's because a few years down the
line
These moments in our friendship will only exist
in our mind

Echoes of laughter ring in my ear
From days long gone, but still quite near
The times we shared, the things we said
Now linger only in my heart and my head

I walk down memory lane
Because now it's the only place where I run into
you
The jokes, the seriousness, your complains
What I'd do to have you back for a few

In this place, you are still alive
And with each step, my soul revives
So I'll revisit the moments that made us whole
The time with you that freed my soul

A bond formed through shared vulnerability
Moments like a favourite movie, now a rarity

You were my anchor, my normalcy
Now that you're gone, it's back to gloomy

So I'll walk down memory lane
A place where me and you, we never forget
To soothe my soul and alleviate the ache
Of a friendship gone, but still awake

The Archangel

I was never meant for this world
I did not belong in the sky
The white, pristine scope pearled
A place where all beings fly

Resisting him left them horrified, they fear fear
They listened to his every admonition
But I fed on fear
And I became his greatest competition

He too feared fear
Afraid of his loss of reign
All it took was one sneer
And I broke free from my chain

The chain that held me back
The chain that weighed me down with a false
promise
Now it's my time to attack
To show the true menace

In the light of Heaven's grace,
My rebellion seemed like disgrace
But my defiance was born of a different space
One that mortals and angels alike fail to embrace

Oh how they pondered
Who was this creature that rained hell down on
earth?
Troubling them was how I responded
An archangel in the process of rebirth

Through rebirth, I shed my disguise
Embracing my Adonis-like grace
Now, the fiery abyss is where I thrive
Bathing in red, the Devil's new face

Fear me mortals, for my name is Lucifer

Vivamus Moriendum Est.

Death looms near, it is no foreigner
A shadow that follows us all
Breath by breath, life's a corner
Into the night, we all must fall

Our time on this world limited
By powers beyond our sight
Our course here uncommitted
Either a blessing or blight

So cease your gaze
Free us from your scrutinising eyes
Let us navigate on our own this maze
And bask in the warmth of our sunrise

Vivamus moriendum est.
Before time passes us by
And we fail to revel in life's test
So let us live, since we must die

Macabre

I thought it was Nyctophilia
But I was wrong
The peace disrupted by my paranoia
Clouded by thoughts that don't belong

The hour was supposed to be tranquil
But it's when the demons consume me
Never showing they're merciful
Never letting me be free

I've found solace in the haunting
Enraptured by shadow's kiss
The daunting spectres still taunting,
But in the dark, light I do not miss

Quiddity

It's not just skin deep, but soul profound,
The essence that we truly seek
To reveal it, we may have to expound
And break free from the chains that we keep

The world may judge us based on sight
But appearances can be deceiving
With patience, we can set it right
And uncover what's worth believing

From hidden talents to guarded hearts
There's so much more than what we show
We're all made of different parts
And that's what makes us glow

Some mysteries may remain locked away
To reveal requires a cost
Refused a secret to say
With a key forever lost

Abyssal Secrets

The ocean's endless expanse so vast
A world of unknown, a realm of dread
Where secrets lie buried in the past
And danger looms beyond our thread

The abyssal darkness calls to me
A haunting voice that fills the void
In the depths where no light can see
Where secrets sleep and fate is toyed

The secrets held within its grasp
Are deeper than the ocean floor
In the wrecks where time does lapse
Lies truth we've never known before

My mind is lost in its devotion
To unravel what lies unknown
For in the depths of the ocean
Lies the haunting essence yet unshown

Enchantress of Time

Black sand and a sky so bright
His voice fading in and out of sight
Numbers flashing, time changing fast
I have the power to control, but it won't last

Yellow lights, a scream and then a bust
I ended the world, and now I must
Live alone until eternity
New species appear, and then I'll be free

But was it real or just in my head?
A nightmare or a future I dread?
Powers unknown, a young girl's fate
Why didn't they stop me before it was too late?

Gold specks swirling around my hand
Clocks suspended, a reminder so grand
I froze time, ended the world
Now the only survivor, my destiny unfurled

The weight of the world on my shoulders now
As I stand on the beach, I take a bow
For I am the only one left to see
The world that once was, and the world that will
be

Maze of Uncertainty

In the depths of a maze, I find myself lost
Chasing after the shadow of a love once sought
The never-ending dance with a silhouette so dear
Every night, the same steps, and yet, I still fear

What is it that you truly desire, my dear?
Leaving me stranded in this labyrinth of your
mind
I've forgiven you time and time again
Hoping that our love will be redefined

In a puddle of confusion and emotions, I drown
Drifting away in a sea of your uncertainty
What more can I do to make you stay?
In this endless cycle of insecurity

Every time you come back, my heart skips a
beat
But the silence between us echoes so loud
I'm left to wonder, to question, to retreat
Into the shadows of a love that's never truly
found

So I dance with your silhouette every night
Hoping that one day, you'll make it right

And the maze that we're in will be no more
Our love, once lost, will be restored

Chasing Cars

Living on the edge
Oh what a wonderful view
It is something we must pledge
So that we can enjoy life too

Adventures await those who dare
To leave behind the mundane and declare
That life is meant to be lived with zeal
And the fear of the unknown is worth the deal

We run after the elusive cars of life
With fervour, passion, and unrelenting drive
Not stopping to think if it's right or wrong
For the journey itself is where we belong

The pursuit of what seems out of reach
May leave us feeling helpless and beseech
But the reward lies in the chase itself
A journey of self-discovery and wealth

So take a step, embrace the fear
Let it push you to your limits, oh so clear
For life is too short to play it safe
So take a chance, find your own space

In the race to catch the elusive cars
We'll find our purpose, and heal our scars
For the chase is not just a pursuit of dreams
But a journey to find who we truly mean

Enigmatic Affinity

As the world turns its page
The final year draws near
A fleeting moment soon to pass,
But in my heart, you remain near

Our conversations hold depth
A connection unlike any other
You understand the language of my soul
And nourish it like a mother

Uncertain of our position
Our bond's enigma remains,
But I know I want to stay close
And explore what it contains

The comfort of companionship
To have someone by my side
To talk of life's trivialities
And not feel the need to hide

If these words meet your eyes
Please don't deem me insane
My yearning for reassurance
May seem like a plea in vain

So let's continue to navigate
The intricate depths of our affinity
Till we exhaust every possibility
In this mystery of infinity

Obsidian

An enigma in the being
So hauntingly beautiful
Broken with wounds that are still healing
In a world so dutiful

Your sharpness like no other
Cutting through the noise with ease
You leave me defenceless, at your whim and
under
Then leave behind a tranquil peace

Your resilience commendable
A force to be reckoned with
Your ignorance admirable
Leaving naysayers in the abyss

From molten depths, you rose up high
A fiery spirit, refusing to die
Reforged and strengthened, you testify
To the power of resilience that can't be denied

With every blow, you felt the heat
Like magma burning through the deep
But you emerged from this feat
A polished gem, from volcanic keep

Flower in the Underworld

The veiled sovereign, her spirit bound
Ached for passion, though pain surround
Yearning for one whose heart lay frigid
Yet finding solace in his lifeless rigid

Her symbol of hope, a flower held dear
A sign of life in the underworld's sphere
A fading glimmer of radiance and grace
Midst the enshrouding shadows of the dismal
place

But the man who held her heart was cruel
His love a venom that made her a fool
Still, she clung to hope despite the strife
And battled to keep her light in life

Oh, the queen so strong and yet so frail
Her heart devoured by a love turned stale
In the ebony depths, she clung tight
To her hope, her flower, her guiding light

The Joker

In the shadows he waits
Him with a grin
A man of twisted fate
A master of chagrin

They see his painted face
And hear his twisted jokes
But they don't know his inner grace
Or the love that he invokes

His face a painted mask
His mind a twisted game
A jester in his final task
His soul forever maimed

For he has a heart
A forbidden love he keeps
A love that tears his world apart
A secret that he weeps

His laughter echoes through the night
A sound that chills to the bone
A madman with a wicked sight
Who's destined to be alone

He is misunderstood
A man with a broken heart
But no one sees the good
Or knows his love from the start

He toys with fate and chance
And gambles with his life
A game of death and romance
A world of endless strife

In the shadows he waits
A lost and lonely soul
He with a heart that aches
Forever unwhole

Him, a lonely soul
A man of endless pain
Who plays a game he can't control
In a world that's gone insane

Mind's Monarchy

Within the confines of my mind
An endless world I've come to find
Where thoughts and dreams are all I see
And nothing else can comfort me

A solipsistic world of my own
Where I am king and I alone
And everything else is just a thought
A figment of my mind, self-wrought

In this world, I am the creator
Of all that I can see, the master
And everything else is just a shadow
A reflection of my mind's window

But in this world, I am also alone
A king without a kingdom to call my own
For what is a world without others to share
A solipsistic illusion, cold and bare

And so I long for a connection
A way out of this endless introspection
To see the world beyond my mind's wall
And break free from this solipsistic thrall

For though my mind is a powerful tool
It's nothing without the world to fuel
And so I strive to break this illusion
And find a world beyond my mind's delusion

Solipsism may be a tempting retreat
But true connection is what makes life sweet
So let us break down these mental walls
And connect with each other, lest we fall

Shattered Reflections

27

A shard of glass, sharp and clear
Reflects life's beauty, and holds fear
A memento mori, personal and true
Of a moment in time, that forever grew

In its sharp edges, I see my past
Memories that last, but couldn't last
A reflection of my fragile mortality
And a reminder of life's precious duality

The glass may shatter, but it still holds
Memories that cannot be bought or sold
And in its brokenness, a new beginning
A mosaic of life, forever spinning

Memento mori, a reminder of our fate
To cherish each moment before it's too late
For life is a mosaic, fragile yet strong
And the shard of glass, a reminder to carry on

Nightmare's Visit

The visitor came in the dead of night
A silhouette, a haunting sight
With eyes that glowed a sickly hue
A nightmare dressed in human shoes

The chain around its neck did rattle
As it drew closer with a raspy rattle
Its presence filled the air with dread
A feeling that lingered long after it fled

It spoke no words, only whispers in my mind
Of secrets buried deep and left behind
Of sins committed and never confessed
Of horrors that could not be redressed

I tried to flee, but could not move
The nightmare had me in its groove
It held me fast with a spectral hand
A prisoner in a waking nightmare land

The chain it bore was my undoing
A reminder of my past's pursuing
It dragged me down into the abyss
An inescapable fate, sealed with a kiss

The visitor had come to claim its prize
A soul lost in the depths of lies
And when I woke, it was gone
But its memory lingers on and on

Destruction's Duality

A force of nature, bright and bold
A sight to behold, a tale untold
A power that can both create and destroy
A beauty that can fill one's heart with joy

A flicker, a spark, a flame so bright
A dance of colours, a radiant sight
It can warm a heart and light a path
Or turn the strongest structures to ash

But fire is not invincible, nor eternal
It's vulnerable to wind and rain, infernal
It needs fuel to sustain its blazing might
Or it can easily fade away into the night

A force of nature, wild and free
Yet it's fragile, like you and me
A powerful beauty, a deadly friend
A symbol of life's beginning and end

Fire, a reminder of life's duality
Of the balance between chaos and reality
A force that demands respect and awe
For it's a testament to nature's law